MATSU

San Diego terroir meets Japanese cuisine

By William Eick

California has the best Japanese restaurants in America. This is a fact. It's no accident that the Michelin Guide has recognized more Japanese restaurants than any other category in the state. And Matsu is better than many of those with the most stars. Or at least different. This isn't sushi. Eick doesn't attempt kaiseki. However, he is the only person cooking like this — and it is extraordinary

- Brad Johnson, December 10, 2023: Matsu

Preface

"I thought this was a Japanese restaurant? Where are your sushi rolls?" These questions from guests, typically the uninformed or unaware types, have been both exceedingly disappointing, and intriguing all at the same time. Ignorance is bliss as they say. But what we do at Matsu, is much much more in depth, and researched, than what the standard "American" thinks is Japanese food. Technically speaking, ramen came over from China, influenced by noodles. Tempura is of Portuguese influence. Sushi, again Chinese influence from a dish called narezushi, which dates back as far as 2nd century BC, and didnt come to Japan until 8th century, roughly the year 718, when it appeared in the Yoro Code.

Food influence can come from anywhere. And within this book, I hope to educate, enlighten, and inspire. To provide what will show that there is MUCH more to Japanese cuisine, and why basing it off our Southern Californian terroir, is paramount to cooking Japanese at the highest level.

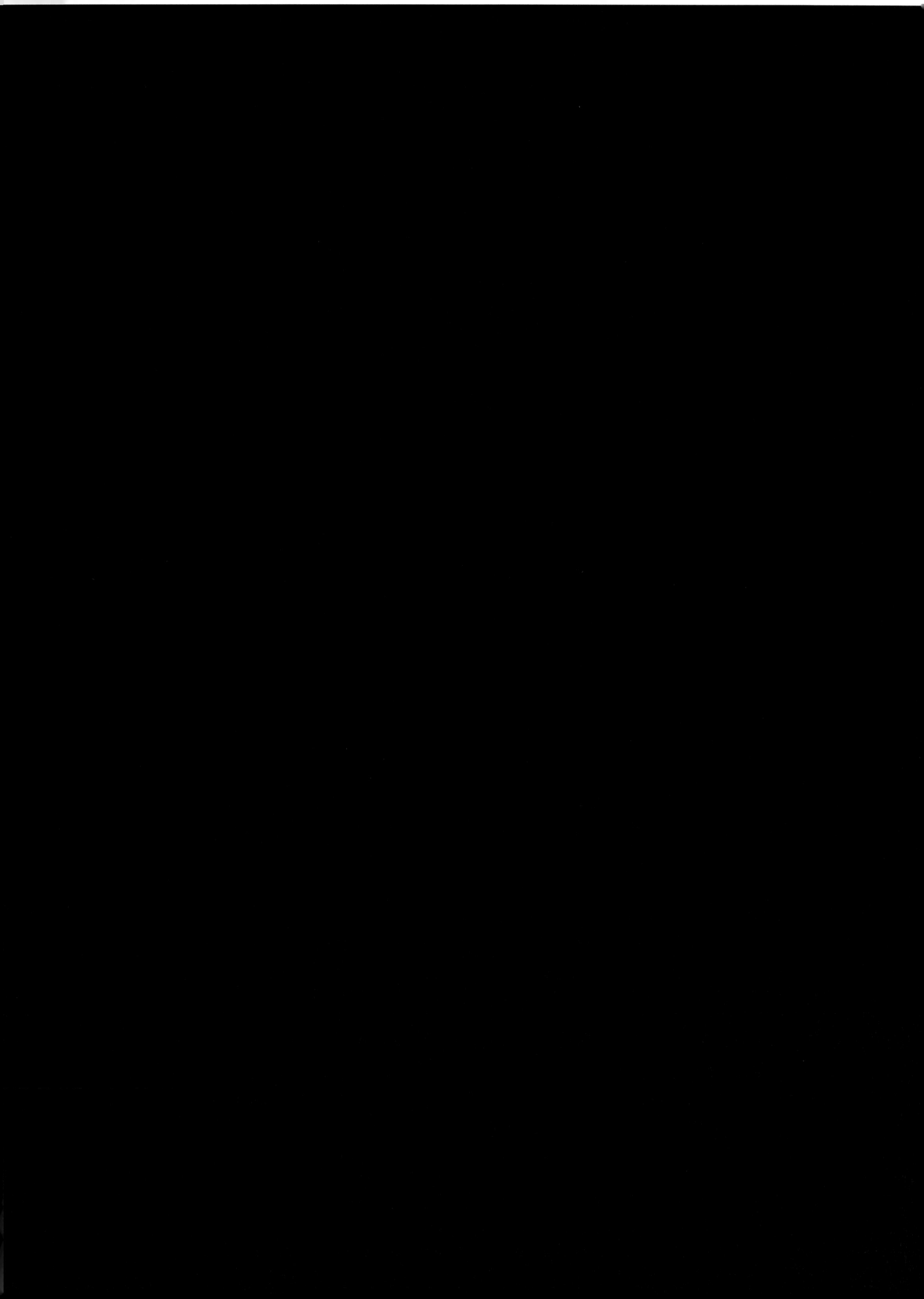

A brief history of Japanese food, culturally

Let us begin with Japanese cuisine, or "washoku" is listed as one of three UNESCO heritage cuisines. The others being French (gastronomy) and Mexican cuisine. It was added to the list in 2013, and Japan holds more 3 Michelin starred restaurants than another other country, and Tokyo is the city with the most in the world as well. The deep roots of tradition, attention to details, and constant pursuit of perfection are things that are deeply rooted in Japanese culture. There is a word for it even. Kaizen, or "constant improvement".

Washoku, or traditional Japanese cuisine, is practiced more socially, and dietary culture that focuses on and emphasizes a use of local ingredients and a deep respect for nature. It involves a passing down of knowledge and skills, by means of a shared meal. Matsu embodies this philosophy. We do our best to educate the guest on what they are about to enjoy, and provide them with a knowledge of ingredients, cooked in a respectful way, and allow the guest to share our journey of constant improvement.

Rice is an absolute staple in Japanese cuisine. Rice would become the staple food of the Japanese people during the Yayoi Period (around 400 BC) at the conclusion of the Jomon Period, and the Japanese food preparation style that uses rice as the staple cuisine item with side dishes of meat and fish was established at that time. Wheat and soybeans were introduced shortly after rice, and all three act as the staples of the cuisine. Without them, we wouldn't have the variety of flavors, dishes, and beverages that we know today. It takes rice to make sake, miso paste, and many other dishes. Soybeans, not just by themselves, are required for miso and soy sauce. Not all, but most soy sauces require the addition of wheat to make, tamari being that outlier. Three very important ingredients used to make many things.

The pre-historical Jomon Period, which lasted from 11000 BC to 600 BC, was the hunting and gathering era before agriculture was introduced to Japan from continental Asia.

During this period, people mainly lived by hunting animals and fish, harvesting nuts and fruits, and so on. Pottery first appeared in Japan at this time, and it allowed for the the cooking method of "simmering" to become possible for the first time.

At the end of the Kofun Period and beginning of the Asuka Period, Buddhism became the official religion of Japan. Eating meat and fish then became prohibited, and Japan became largely vegetarian. Because of this, there resulted in a minimized use of spice. Peppers and garlic became only slightly used. By the end of the Asuka Period, roughly early 8th century, fish started to be eaten, even though many emperors continued to prohibit the killing of many other animals, which let to further banning mammals, except whales (which they categorized as fish). Fish became the main source of protein, and in the 9th century, it was popular to eat it grilled, or sliced and enjoyed raw. It was natural for Japanese to avoid things like oils and fats during the cooking process in order to keep a more healthy lifestyle.

Narezushi became a sensation. Originally, it was a means of preserving fish, by fermenting it in boiled rice to help prevent bacteria growth that would otherwise bring about putrefaction. During the 15th century, improvements and development had helped speed up with fermentation, requiring only one to two weeks time. It resulted in making the "sushi" a popular snack at the time, especially when consumed with rice. During the late Edo period (late 19th century), sushi without fermentation was introduced, though it was still enjoyed either fermented or not, in either nigiri or handroll (temaki) form. It is worth noting at this point that sushi "rolls" are not Japanese, but as sushi moved from Japan, to Canada, then to the United States, it was modified to fit the American Palate. There are a few "maki" rolls you would see in Japan, but nothing like what Americans mostly associate with sushi rolls.

Around the mid 1600's, foreign trade came under strict government control, and the Tokugawa policy of national isolation was complete. This resulted in external influences ceasing and Japan entered a phase of refinement and maturity within itself, which lasted for about 200 years.

It wasn't until the Meiji Restoration when the government began to adopt Western customs, including the use of animal products in food. In 1872, the new ruler staged a New Years feast designed to reflect more of a European diet, and for the first time in over a thousand years, people were allowed to consume meat in public, resulting in it becoming a regular part of their diets. The removal of the ban on the consumption of red meats, resulting in some resistance, and monks asserted that foreign influence and meat eating was "destroying the soul of the Japanese".

"Kare Raisu", or Curry Rice, wasn't introduced to Japan until the mid 1800's, though has been dated as far back as 1772, even if it were misspelled in books (usually spelled as Taisu Kare). The first known recipe dates 1872, from Kanagaki Robun, and the Japanese Army Military Academy followed serving it the following year. It is thought to have been brought over and introduced by British Navy, after having stopped in India, has become one of Japan's most popular dishes, and ranks near the top of nearly all Japanese favorite food surveys. The origin however, is linked to what is called "yoshoku", or western cuisine. Yoshoku can be found as far back as the Muromachi period. This was first seen in Nagasaki, and spread outwards until it became popular during the Meiji period, considered the be the first time Japan opened itself to the outside world.

I think its worth mentioning that "kappo" is another term associated with "cooking", much used in the Meiji and Taisho eras, as a reference to Japanese cooking, or restaurants. It is generally seen as a slightly more casual eating establishment compared to kaiseki.

Kaiseki, which actually translates to "warming stone", is more tied with the Japanese tea ceremony, and also considered a more simplified form of "honzen-ryori" (main tray cooking), formal banquet dining where several trays of food are served. To say we serve kaiseki at Matsu (which has been said a few times, though not often), would be incorrect, especially if you look at the literal translations. Even then, kaiseki meals tend to follow a strict progression of dishes, and that is not something we intentionally follow either, though kaiseki is associated with a high form of hospitality, so I do see a connection from the guest perspective.

As with most restaurants these days, there has also always been an emphasis placed upon the seasonality of foods, and in Japanese this is called "shun". Seasonality can be found in just about every culture, though the Japanese break it down into as much as seventy two micro seasons. If something becomes available earlier than what is typically expected, the first crop, or catch if it is fish, is called "hashiri".

Ramen, at least the word itself, only first appeared in 1928, when Seiichi Yoshida's book, "How to Prepare Delicious and Economical Chinese Dishes" was published. In this case, it more refers to the noodles, and not the the dish itself. The dish was mentioned much later, in 1947. Prior to that, ramen-like dishes were referred to by other names, one being Chuka

Soba (Chinese noodles), but most commonly it was "Shina soba", however that name holds an association with anti-Chinese racism and Japanese imperialism, so it isn't used much today, resulting in "Ramen" being widely used. Ramen is thought to have first appeared in Yokohama's Chinatown.

Bread is not a traditional food, but was later developed and came into a more common usage due to the American response to post World War II Japanese rice shortages. Most commonly known as "shokupan" Japanese Milk Bread has recently gained popularity around the world.

Matsu: The Restaurant

Matsu is, in its decor, very minimalist. There isn't really much to it. Although we were on a tight budget from the start, we tried to make sure we kept the attention to detail in the necessary things, and left out anything we deemed unnecessary. There are a few wood shelves that hold small plants, and on occasion small bonsai, a wooden server station, black walnut tables, and walnut chairs. Most of the walls are simply grey, with a few paintings on the larger "empty" spaces. One wall was left untouched, because it look as if it were large concrete slabs. We opened the kitchen up, and created the "Chef's Counter", and epoxied the floor to look as if it were wood as well. We wanted it to feel and look like something you would find in Japan. The door is solid black walnut, and the few windows have blackout curtains.

When you enter Matsu, especially during the early evening when the sun is still out, it is almost blinding. The dim lit dining room is almost pitch black for the first few seconds, until your eyes adjust, and if you finish your experience early enough, when you walk back outside, it again is somewhat blinding for a few seconds. We actually anticipated this reaction both times, for several reasons. The first is because right as service starts, the sun is nearing the ocean on the west side, and does create a lot of light inside. So much so, it would be both very hot, and very blinding. Instead of shades, we decided black out curtains would be best, which allows us to keep the same lighting all service. Secondly, the pure shock of the bright to dark, subconsciously resets the guests mindset. It allows us to "transport" the guest to a different world, removing their worries, giving them a fresh start, and allowing them to focus on their experience with us at Matsu.

Our service is seemingly simple. We give the guest what is necessary to begin the experience, do our best to anticipate any guests needs, and allow the guests to enjoy their company. If guests seem like they want longer, more in depth explanations of dishes, or beverages, we provide them with the information. If guests seem to want to only enjoy the company they came with, we do our best to become subtle and non-distracting. Every guest is different, and we try to keep each experience specific to each group. Every course is met with new cutlery, the duck and wagyu allowing the guests to choose from a selection of custom made knives.

Matsu: The Food

Matsu means "pine" in Japanese. I chose Matsu because the deeply rooted history of pine in Japanese culture, and the local Torrey Pine trees that San Diego is known for. Matsu is about the traditions and culinary techniques of Japanese culture and cuisine, and marrying them with our terroir of southern California. The more I think of Matsu and pine trees, the more I find it relates to myself as well. My last name, Eick, originally is from Eichman, which means people of the (oak) trees in German. My wife's fathers side originally came from China, immigrating through Southeast Asia, through the Pacific, before making it to Oceanside, and they stopped at an island named "Matsu" along the way. Trees, and Matsu itself, has places throughout my life.

The food at Matsu is seemingly simple yet very much fitting to my personality. As a highly introverted person, the plates looking quiet, minimal, and subtle. Once you eat the food however, it is loud, in your face flavor, not holding anything back. When I do something, I want it to be the best. Perfection does not exist, yet Im always pushing for it. My mother used to tell me when I was a swimmer and Id be upset about losing a race, that there is always someone better and to not dwell on it. That stuck with me, and gave me the motivation to continue striving to always be better. Our goal for Matsu is to be the best Matsu we can, serve the best food we can possibly cook, and improve each day.

Ive never been one to hold back when it comes to my food. Ive probably over-seasoned probably more times than Ive been under. I push the salt and acid levels right to the edge. I want the guest to taste the course they just finished all the way until their next course enters their mouth. I want them to remember their meal for weeks to months, if not for years to come. This book is about Matsu up to its current point. It is a look into the thoughts behind the dishes, and to show how simple truly delicious food can be. It is all about product, and sourcing the best you can possibly get. Understanding flavor profiles of some odd, and some common ingredients and matching them accordingly. It is about balance. The balance of flavor profiles in order to create and retain depth. Not just salt and acid, but also sweet, bitter, and importantly, the true meaning of umami. Umami is the most overused, and least understood flavor, especially by American chefs. Umami should give you a sense of fullness. Not in your stomach, but in your mouth. On your palate. You should more than taste it, you should feel it coat your mouth. When tasting some of the sauces on their own from this book, remember those words, and I promise it will all begin to make sense.

The sauces, and dashi are much about temperature control. Something to remember as you work through each one, most of them are treated more like tea than how you would cook in, say, a French setting. True umami at its best is destroyed the moment the dashi reaches a certain temperature, around 155 degrees Fahrenheit. We do our best to ensure that most don't exceed that number. It also allows us to extract and retain the subtle delicate flavors of the base ingredients, to ensure more depth, better balance, and a more pure flavor. There will be a few exceptions, but for the most part, low and slow is the name of the game when it comes to our cooking.

Why quality ingredients are the most important aspect

Dashi

Dashi is the, lifeblood if you will, of Japanese cooking. It is in Japanese food what stock is to French food, though it is much more simple than a traditional stock. Sometimes as simple as kombu (seaweed), and water. What most don't realize is, dashi in Japan will almost always be better than most other places on the planet. Not because the kombu is a better quality, which more times than not, it can be. What is often overlooked, is the hardness of the water. Japan typically has softer water, which in turn allows more subtle extraction of flavor, and more importantly, umami. Not everything uses dashi as a base, but the way the glutamic acid of the seaweed reacts in softer water, it allows the umami to be more present.

I specifically like Ma kombu from Hokkaido the best, though we also interchange it with Rishiri kombu, also from Hokkaido, if Ma is not available. We then had a special water filtration system put in that allows us to achieve much softer water than we would if we used what comes out of the tap.

At Matsu, we look beyond a simple dashi, sometimes treating sauces in similar fashion, and understanding the temperature "game" that we try to play to push the maximum flavor enjoyment into our food. Sometimes we use clarified tomato juice instead of water, sometimes it is kombu added to the end of the yaki sauces or curries, all in the name of depth and tradition. Starting with a quality dashi, and the best end result becomes much more achievable.

Soy Sauce

Soy sauce can be very much two different experiences based on the quality you use. Generic, commercial soy sauce is, in my opinion, salty brown water. Not much depth, very basic flavor. Not necessarily a bad product, but more often than not, best used for cooking rather than final seasoning.

Making soy sauce can typically take quite a bit of time, so it is not something we currently do ourselves, but we are not opposed to doing it at some point. Mostly, it is soy and wheat made into a patty, then inoculated with koji rice, and left to ferment in a salty brine after it has molded, resulting a "brewing" style of fermentation.

Our main "house" shoyu (another name for soy sauce), is a double brewed shoyu, which the brewery makes the first batch of shoyu, then instead of using water and salt, uses the first shoyu to then brew the second. It is intense in flavor, much more viscous in texture, and surprisingly enough, less salty than regular shoyu. It is perfect for cooking with, though we also use another for cooking as well.

Our other cooking shoyu is Usukuchi shoyu, or light colored shoyu. This time is more specifically used for cooking. It tastes saltier than other shoyu as well, which is a result of it being less aged. Any time we want to braise, or add shoyu to a sauce as a seasoning, and not the main component, this is what we use. Kikkoman makes a commercial version, but we use a small producer out of Tatsuno City, Japan who's quality is unmatched.

Mirin

Mirin, especially here in the States, can be frustrating when trying to find quality product. More often than not, it is a product made from various inverted sugars (glucose, corn syrup, etc) that have koji "enzymes" added to them for flavor. Real mirin, is very similar to sake, in the sense of it is a brewed product, it is rice, koji and water. The main difference from sake to "real" mirin (hon mirin), is the type of rice. Mirin is made with the same rice that mochi is made with, glutinous rice, that hold the higher sugar content resulting in thicker viscosity, and also a nice "shine" a dish as well.

Hon mirin will change the entire understanding of what mirin really is after the first sip of trying it, and the ultimate understanding of why it can and should be used.

Sake

Most will tell you that if you are cooking it, the wine/sake doesn't need to be expensive, and should be the cheapest you can find. I wholeheartedly disagree that the quality doesn't matter. Quality doesn't always equate to the most expensive bottle, but as with anything, quality going in, provides a better chance of quality coming out.

I prefer to use a sake that taste more of shiitake, or really strong umami flavors. Our food is geared towards pushing the maximum flavor, and more often that means we push stronger flavors into each ingredient. A lighter, more fruity flavored sake could work for certain dishes, but most of those, we aren't using sake in.

Sake is also best used when cooking. Similar to wine in most other countries. Occasionally it will be used in marinades, like karaage for example, and rarely, we use it to season something, but that is only when vinegar or some form of citrus juice would be too overbearing.

Sugar (more specifically kokuto)

Kokuto, or Okinawan Brown/Black sugar, is Matsu's most used ingredient. Not cheap by any stretch of the imagination, as far as sugars go, but also, nothing comes close in terms of quality and flavor. Only eight islands in the archipelago produce what can be called Okinawan brown sugar, and each one is different, based off their terroir. Ours comes from Hateruma Island and is highly prized for its earthy tones and savoriness.

It is the base of our yaki glazes, and savory caramels. It shows up in our sorbet and ice cream. Any time we need sugar, with small exceptions, it is our first choice. We even use it for simple syrup for cocktails. We could not achieve the same flavors and depth without it.

Vegetables (and why they deserve the focus over the meat)

Vegetables can be the single biggest surprise to a guest, when cooked properly. At Matsu, we tend to lean into exploring the vegetable in its entirety, especially when we have access to all parts of the plant. Take for example a sunflower; the heart, leaves, stem, roots, pedals, seeds; all edible. Working with each one in a different way, understanding each part has a different, unique flavor, allows us to make one ingredient much more impactful. Not just from a guest perspective, but in terms of depth and flavor. It is a means of true sustainable cooking, no part is wasted, as the indigenous peoples would have done. Unadulterated respect for an ingredient.

Most times, the vegetable itself becomes the focal point of a dish for us, because of that. Then we decide which protein would elevate that experience. Each season, each year, each moment, the same vegetable can change. That to me, is what makes not only being a chef so exciting, but makes the vegetable the most important component on the plate. Never an afterthought. If it doesn't have meaning to be there other being an afterthought, if should be removed. Showing restraint is paramount.

As young chefs, we tend to want to put everything we know onto each plate. The more experience I gain, the more I find it unnecessary to make food that is complicated. Complex food is very much achievable without being overly complicated, and exploring vegetables in their entirety is a way to, in my opinion, find the complex flavors for a dish while keeping it relatively simple.

Meats

Meat quality, to me, can be somewhat subjective. Just because I prefer one cut of an animal over another, doesn't mean the quality itself is better, or worse. I feel, especially in the western world, "quality" cuts are those that "melt in your mouth" and require almost no chewing. Eastern palates will understand, and sometimes celebrate, those lesser cuts, because they have various textures to them. A tenderloin of beef may be very easy to eat, and soft in texture, but in all honestly lacks flavor. Fat, is flavor. It is why we as humans love pork belly, or A5 wagyu from Japan. Tons of fat. I do believe there is a balance to be had, which is why more often I find myself searching for different cuts of A5 (we usually use sirloin these days), because the obvious strip loin and ribeyes lack explosive beef flavor. A sirloin, cooked properly, will have more beef flavor, but also have enough fat in it to provide that sense of luxury.

Another misnomer that I have been seeing more often than not, the most expensive ingredient does not always mean the best quality. Perfect, ika jime rockfish that come into Matsu within hours of being caught and dispatched, will be a much higher quality fish, in terms of freshness, than any fish we might ship from overseas or source from other suppliers.

Yes, there are variances within, which is why when we do source Japan fish, it is because we know the quality of care is much higher, consistently, than what we can get local. I would love to have things like squid from local boats, but the level of care isn't there, yet, to match what Matsu currently gets from Japan.

Climate can change quality as well. Not just in vegetables, but meat as well, and more easily noticeable, fish. Colder waters result in cleaner fish, especially shellfish. I prefer my uni from Hokkaido, over San Diego or even Santa Barbara. Other chefs might prefer the Santa Barbara. That is ok. Personal preference will always exist. With me, for Matsu, I prefer cleaner flavors of colder water uni, as it doesn't have the off mercury, irony finish of the warmer watered local ones.

Other Seasonings

Often the most overlooked aspect of a dish. Dried chilis, sesame seeds (paste and oil as well), kombu, salt, peppercorns, etc, all have different variations of quality. As previously mentioned with things like sugar, soy sauce, etc, it is important to think abut the quality of everything that goes into a dish.

Our sansho peppercorn powder that gets sourced from a very small producer in Japan, is kept in the freezer, as to not lose the fresh, almost lemongrass and verbena nuances, and the vibrant green color, that is has. Even a week at room temperature, and there a vast difference. The subtle southeastern Asian-esc herb profiles are gone, the color is dulled and almost brown. It is not the same as it once was.

Our sesame oil is so clean and pure in flavor, is almost tastes like peanut oil, has no metallic off flavors that is typically found in the normal, readily available at your local grocery outlet, sesame oil does. It is world class. The extra virgin olive oil version of sesame oils. Single pressed. Pure bliss. We typically use it as a finishing oil, though occasionally it will get added to certain sauces (like the rayu).

Finding Balance (in all the ingredients)

Balance. The harmony of all the ingredients coming together to form a thoughtful, layered experience of flavors. As a dish gets seasoned, it should taste of all the things that went into it. Maybe a little more acid, more salt, possibly a touch of something bitter to round things out. Doesn't it actually need some fat incorporated to make those flavors linger? Maybe a pinch of sugar, or something else sweet, to push that much more flavor in?

Then there is umami. I find most people confuse this flavor profile. They don't understand the reaction is has on the palate, just it might mean "delicious, savory taste". Umami, from a palate reaction, is a sense of fullness, or roundness on the tongue. It doesn't make you feel it in just one specific area as does salt, or acid (sour), but makes your whole mouth salivate. Understanding that reaction, will not only help understand umami more intimately, but allow the focus of reaction with the other flavor profiles, resulting in a higher understanding of balance in a dish. Having the other basic flavor profiles in balance, can pull forward the umami a bit more as well, enhancing the reaction on the palate. It is a wonderful thing, but requires a lot of focus, and palate training to understand.

Techniques, and when to show restraint

Restraint is most definitely the largest sign of a good chef. It shows maturity, understanding, and at times, a genius mastery of cookery. Knowing when to hold back and allow the ingredient to be exactly as it is, because it may be perfect in that moment, is something I feel is wholly Japanese from a technical standpoint. Sushi is a wonderful example of this. Perfect fish, on perfectly cooked and seasoned rice. Nothing more. Pure bliss. There is no denying that. At its finest, there is no getting better.

Now, there is a constant wonder of how to improve from that perfect moment, which I also relate to being a mentality the Japanese have (see Kaizen), but in that moment, it should be as good as it can be, given your current knowledge. That daily improvement, even if small, is what makes Matsu what it is. We can cook our recipes to a T daily, but have a constant sense of wonder to make them better, removing any unnecessaries in the process.

As it is said, "Less is more".

The Menu

Menu changes occur typically monthly, with only one dish changing most times. We have been through several format changes, each time, finding out identity and refining it even more. Not just what works best for us, but what works best for the guest as well. Constant improvements are made to better the guest experience. We have our staple dishes, and minor seasonal changes are made to those, to reflect time and place. The recipes that follow show what we would typically serve, and how we make them. They are not adapted to home cooking, and are truly what we use each day.

Otsumami

Otsumami means "snacks". A few bites to the opening course, mostly to allow the guests to enjoy more at the start and not feel rushed or overwhelmed with a quick start to their evening. Sometimes, in Kaiseki format, it could be called "Hassun", though we don't fit the traditional sense of the dish, which is why we went with Otsumami.

Koginut Squash

Miso Mustard (Mix blonde miso, dijon mustard, and sugar to taste)
Seeds
Sunflower Powder
Dried Sunflower Pedals
Ikura

- To order, brûlée a large cube of squash with some white sugar. Spread a thin layer of miso mustard, then finish with the roasted squash seeds, sunflower pedals, powder, and Ikura.

Japanese Milkbread

For the tangzhong

90 grams AP flour
1 cup whole milk

For the dough

650 grams AP flour
120 grams sugar
19 grams fresh yeast (2 packets if dry active)
8 grams sea salt
2 eggs
1 cup warm whole milk, plus extra for brushing on the unbaked loaf
8 tablespoons unsalted butter, cut into pieces and softened at room temperature, plus extra for buttering bowls and pan

Make Starter then reserve. Mix drys in kitchen aid with dough hook, then add wets, and starter. Last, add butter and mix. Portion dough to 20g balls and rise until doubled in size Preheat oven to 325, high fan. Bake 13 minutes. Rest until cool. Keep wrapped in plastic or in airtight container if not using immediately.

- To order, heat in the oven at 325 until soft and warm throughout. Roll in rendered wagyu fat, and finish with maldon sea salt.

Dorayaki

Batter
450g Ap
3tsp Bp
3tsp Bs
120 Sugar
3 egg
600mL milk

Kanpachi | Raspberry | Marigold

Raspberry Ponzu

780g Raspberries
270g Usukuchi Shoyu
3ea Hawk Claw
1g Rice Vinegar
9g Mirin
1ea Kombu
2ea Lime Leaf
15g Lemon Balm

Heat all ingredients except Kombu and Lemon Balm, at very low heat, to infuse the flavors for 20 minutes. Remove from heat, and steep in Kombu and Lemon Balm.

Kanpachi Tartare

Lime Leaf Oil

Assemble: Place tartare at the bottom of the bowl. Mix 6g ponzu with 2g lime leaf oil. Place raspberry pieces and marigold pedals on top.

Sunflower | Ika | Rayu

Rayu
75g sesame oil - roasted
56g green onion
238g grapeseed oil
37g dried shrimp
30g dried squid
25g togarashi
4g thai chili
15g shoyu - aged
54g garlic
166g onion
52g ginger
30g Okinawan brown sugar

Squid sheets
Puree the squid crowns with a little sake and mirin. Spread on a silpat to form a thin sheet and steam in oven at 325 for 5 minutes.

Sunflower Powder

Dehydrate Sunflower leaves (not flower pedals, green leaves) until dried. Blend to a powder.

To Assemble
Fry the cuttlefish tentacles with potato starch. Meanwhile dust one side of a 5x5 squid sheet with the sunflower leaf powder. Flip over and place 5 pieces of diced sunflower heart, cover with rayu, then a few dots of sweet potato vinegar gel, then seeds, then fresh sunflower pedals and finally the fried tentacles. Wrap as you would temaki, or a handroll.

Sunflower Powder

Dehydrate Sunflower leaves (not flower pedals, green leaves) until dried. Blend to a powder.

To Assemble - Fry the cuttlefish tentacles with potato starch. Meanwhile dust one side of a 5x5 squid sheet with the sunflower leaf powder. Flip over and place 5 pieces of diced sunflower heart, cover with rayu, then a few dots of sweet potato vinegar gel, then seeds, then fresh sunflower pedals and finally the fried tentacles. Wrap as you would temaki, or a handroll.

Roasted Seeds
500g Sunflower Seeds
5g Grapeseed Oil
Sea Salt TT

Sweet Potato Vinegar Gel
Sweet Potato Vinegar
Ultratex

Sheer in ultratex using a food processor until fluid gel forms.

Sunflower Hearts
Kinpira Liquid, to cover
Sunflower Hearts

Simmer until the liquid has reduced to a syrup, and the sunflower hearts are no longer bitter

Ebi Tempura | Tentsuyu | Dynamite

Tempura Batter

4c Pastry Flour
1c Potato Starch
Ice cold water, to desired thickness

Tentsuyu

68g shoyu
22g Okinawan brown sugar
333g shrimp dashi
44g mirin
27g ginger
39g green onion
.25g chili flake
1g Szechuan peppercorns

Shrimp Dashi

45g shells
850g water
1 kombu sheet

Matsu Dynamite

235g Kewpie
25g rayu
3g salt
3 each Thai chili
7g honey
35g Masago
7g garlic, fresh grated

To Assemble - Fry the ebi in the batter, reserving the tenkasu. Once cooked, coat one side with the dynamite, then crust with the tenkasu. Season with golden sesame oil, and togarashi, then finish with tentsuyu.

Lobster | Abalone | Sweet Potato

Lobster Dashi

65g Lemongrass
275g Onion
28g Ginger
24g Garlic
70g Sake
70g Usukuchi Shoyu
110g Mirin (white bottle hon mirin)
185g Tomato Paste
350g Lobster Shells
1.5qt Water
1ea Chili
30g Kombu
7g Curry Leaf

Sweat the lemongrass, garlic, ginger, and onion in grapeseed oil with a pinch of salt. Once fragrant, add lobster shells, and caramelize. Once the shells are cooked and color has changed, add the sake, shoyu and mirin. Reduce by half, then add tomato paste, stir and cook for 1 minute, then add water and chili. Simmer 30 minutes, until slightly reduced, then steep in kombu and curry leaves for 1 hour. Strain.

Abalone Liver Glaze

10 livers
4tbsp Sake
2tbsp Mirin
3tbsp Usukuchi
2tbsp Oki
1L abalone cooking liquid

Pan roast the livers then deglaze with sake soy mirin and oki sugar. Then blend corn into cooking liquid then reduce until glaze thickness. When cooled season with Aged Shoyu and salt until balanced

Sweet Potato Dashi

1.7L Juiced Sweet Potato
4g Szechuan Peppercorn
3 Hawk Claw Chili
2 Bay Leaf
3 Kinome
Handful Curry Leaf
4 Green Onion Whites
10g Sweet Potato Vinegar
2 Kombu
Salt and Whiskey Barrel Soy TT

Juice sweet potato and add Chilis. Heat on electric stove top at 120 Degrees. Make sure to whisk every few minutes to prevent starch from clumping on the bottom of the pan. Once sauce has been hot for about 30 minutes remove from heat. After heating Steep in remaining ingredients for 1hr. Strain through strainer with the largest holes. Season to taste.

Lobster "Chowder"

210g Lobster Dashi
220g Sweet Potato Dashi
20g Blonde Miso
25g Abalone, diced
4g Chive
1g Truffle Zest

Heat both dashi and miso together in a pot and whisk until thickened. Dice then grill the abalone, glazing with the liver sauce to provide char. Remove from heat and stir in grilled abalone, chives and truffle. Season to taste.

Ti Leaf Oil

500g Grapeseed Oil
100g Ti Leaves

Freeze the oil. Blanch the leaves, then blend the leaves with the frozen oil on high until the oil "steams". Strain through linen/cheese cloth to remove any solids.

Abalone Cooking Liquid

Abalone
Shiitake Dashi

Pressure cook the abalone in shiitake dashi at 10 lbs of pressure for 45 minutes in a pressure cookers.

To Assemble - Grill this lobster tail with lobster shell oil. Slice into 2 pieces, and place on the chowder and finish with ti leaf oil and lobster oil.

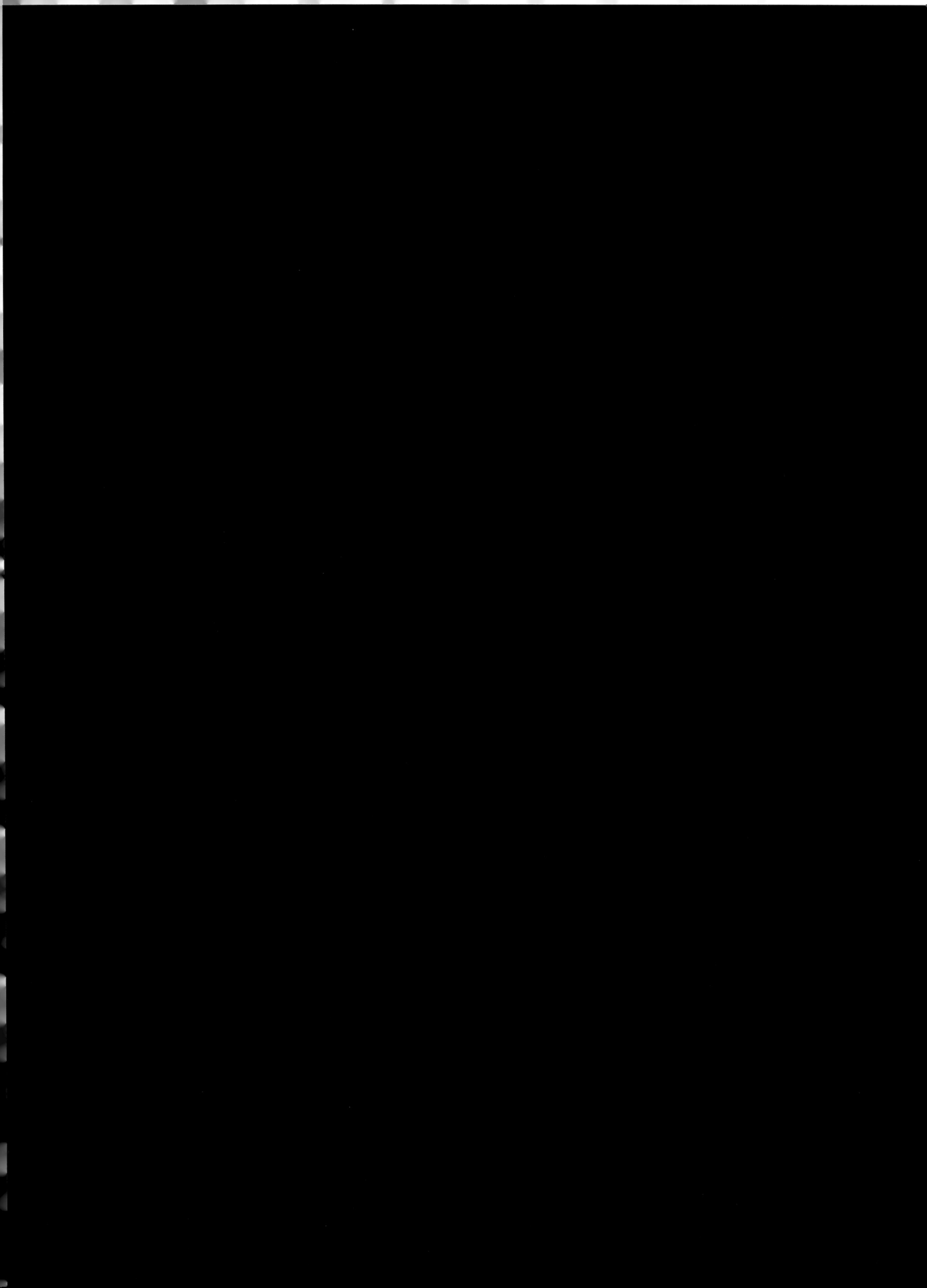

Oyakodon

Chicken Onion Jam

676g Whites of Green Onion
50g Brown Sugar
185g Chicken Floss Cooking Liquid
454g Green Onion Greens
Salt TT

Caramelize white of onions with sugar. Then deglaze with chicken floss cooking liquid and add green onions. Reduce and caramelize again until the spiciness of onions is gone and then season with salt.

Chicken Floss

5lb Chicken Thigh
Kinpira Liquid to cover
7g Fish Sauce
10g Usukuchi Shoyu
10g Kokuto Syrup

Rendered Chicken Fat

1lb Chicken Skin

Chicken Dashi Foam

500g Roasted Chicken Dashi
6g Lecithin Powder

Ramen Cured Egg yolk

2c Mirin
1c Usukuchi Shoyu
Yolks (as many as needed)

Koshihikari Rice

1qt rice
.9qt water

Cover the defrosted chicken thighs in the Kinpira recipe to be found in sauté section. Bring to a simmer and skim the scum. Once the thighs are fully cooked strain and reserve the cooking liquid for the onion jam. Shred the thighs and toss with the liquid seasonings place in a thin layer on a sheet tray. Bake at 250 for 30-60mins. Once dry pulse the floss in a food processor and season with salt.

To Assemble - Heat the rice with the rendered chicken fat. Place in the bowl and add the onion jam in the middle. Add the chicken floss around the jam, and garnish with bachelor button flowers on the floss. Add a cured egg yolk on the jam, then cover everything with chicken dashi foam.

Duck | Tsukune | Matsuyaki

Duck Leg Tsukune

55g Leg Meat
1g Salt
2g Green Onion, White Only
5g Wasabi
5g Tare

Grind meat, then mix well. Portion to 2oz, and bake for 7 minutes at 325. Once cool, dust with flour then dip in whisked eggs then coat with panko to make the Katsu.

Matsuyaki

480g okinawan brown sugar
600g double brewed shoyu
172g duck bones, roasted
5 dried chili
5g cilantro stems
2 sprig kinome
5g rice vinegar
1 sheet kombu
1 bunch green onion, tops only
8 verbena leaves
1 Tbsp Szechuan peppercorns

Steam the shoyu, sugar, chili flake and duck bones at 140 degrees until reduced by 1/4, steep in remaining ingredients for 1 hour then strain.

To Assemble - Render the fat from the skin side of the duck breast. Then, marinate the duck breast in Shio koji for 30 minutes. Dry the breast, then season with sea salt on the flesh side only. Roast at 325, fan high for 10 minutes. Once rested, grill to medium while glazing with Matsuyaki sauce then rest. Meanwhile, fry the Tsukune Katsu until deep golden brown and cooked through. Grill a few brassica leaves for garnish. Place a quenelle of the Kosho, and garnish with a slice of fresh kumquat.

Wagyu | Onion | Sukiyaki

Sukiyaki Sauce

120g sake
268g mirin
94g n brown sugar
417g shoyu
20g rice vinegar
3g Szechuan peppercorns
5ea hawk claw chili
4g katsuobushi
20g ginger, grated
10g garlic, grated
2g hojicha
20g white miso
1 sheet kombu
Wagyu trim, roasted

Melt the sugar in the sake, mirin, shoyu, peppercorns, chili, vinegar and roasted wagyu trim. Remove from heat and steep in remaining ingredients for 1 hour. Strain.

Caramelized Onion

110g onion
10g okinawan brown sugar
20g grapeseed
4g rice vinegar
2g Mizunara shoyu
2g salt

In a pan, begin to sweat the shallots in grapeseed until translucent. Add sugar and begin to caramelize. Once deep brown, deglaze with a light amount of vinegar. Mix then remove from heat. Once negi has cooled to room temp, season with shoyu and salt to taste.

To Assemble - Grill 2.5oz Wagyu to medium, glazing with Matsuyaki to provide caramelization on the meat. While resting, season with Sansho peppercorn powder. Meanwhile place onions in the bowl, and sprinkle masago arare on them. Place the wagyu on top, then add freshly grated wasabi. Finish the plate with a spoon full of sukiyaki sauce.

Pine | Cherry | Chocolate

Rehydrated Cherries

1000g Dried cherries
300mL sake
240g Okinawan brown sugar syrup
24g sakura shoyu
5 kinome

Simmer the cherries with the sugar, sake and miso until cherries are cooked through. Mix in kinome, and Shoyu. Steep until needed.

Pine/Yuzu Sorbet

1qt Pine Needle Juice (blend 70g needles with 952g water, strain)
1qt Yuzu Juice
1118g White Sugar
200g Okinawan Brown Sugar
4 Drops Green Food Coloring
2g Salt

Chocolate Soil

112g butter
64g Okinawan brown sugar
160g cocoa powder
2g Cinnamon
1g Szechuan
1g Cardamon
4.8g salt
36g eggs white (1)

mix the sugar, cocoa powder, and spices in a in food processor until broken up. Add butter and egg whites, rest for 1 hour, bake at 325 for 15 minutes, cool in the walk in, then crumble (hands work best, its soft).

Combine all ingredients except for yuzu juice and white sugar in a blender. Blend to a pulp and then strain off into container. Add white sugar and yuzu then whisk until all sugar is melted. Then spin in the ice cream machine for 7 mins at first. Check how frozen it is. The goal is to have firm peaks of sorbet.

To Assemble - At the bottom of the bowl, plate the soil, then add the rehydrated cherries, then dust with cherry blossom powder. Finish with a rocher of sorbet.

Miso | White Chocolate | Tangerine

Blonde Miso/Vanilla Ice Cream

2qt Heavy Cream
1qt Milk
500g white sugar
100g Okinawan Brown Sugar
360g Yolks
200g White Miso
21g Hokkaido Milk Powder
7g Vanilla

Heavy milk, cream and sugar until simmer. Ladle 12oz hot milk into a mixing bowl with the yolks and whisk to temper the yolks. Once tempered, slowly pour the yolks while whisking, into the pot with the milk on low heat. Continue to whisk until liquid is nape (slightly thickened). Remove from heat, strain through chinois, and mix in remaining ingredients.

Orange Dashi Gel

9g sesame seeds
9g star anise
690g orange juice
105g orange blossom water
2ea kinome
3g lemon balm
1 sheet kombu
4g sakura shoyu
1g salt
6g mirin

Heat sesame, anise, orange juice, and orange water until light simmer starts and pulp has separated. Steep in kinome, lemon balm, and kombu 1 hour. Strain through like linen, then season with salt, mirin and shoyu. Place in food processor and sheer in ultratex until fluid gel is formed.

Caramelized White Chocolate

1000g White Chocolate
10g Hokkaido Milk Powder

Bake the white chocolate at 325 degrees, fan high, stirring every 5 minutes until caramelized. Remove from oven and with a rolling pin, spread as thin as possible between two sheet pan liners. Place in fridge until solid, then spread milk powder on the sheets.

To assemble - Dress segments of Kishu tangerine with the orange blossom gel. Place a scoop of the ice cream in the middle, then cover it with abstract pieces of caramelized white chocolate.

Wagashi

Kokuto Jelly

1818g water
1238g Kokuto
18g agar

Heat in a pot until boils, stirring occasionally so it doesn't boil over, to melt the agar and sugar. Pour into a plastic wrap lined half sheet pan and set in the walk in.

Castella Cake

231g egg white
100g sugar

103g egg yolk
80mL whole milk
80g grapeseed oil
40g mochiko
90g pastry flour
1g salt
5g vanilla paste

Whip the egg whites in a stand mixer until medium stiff peaks, adding the sugar in 1/3 at a time during the whipping process. Reserve for later. Meanwhile, mix remaining ingredients in a separate bowl, starting with the drys then adding the wets. Fold in the meringue into the batter. Line a quarter sheet pan with a silpat, and bake at 325 degrees, fan on high, for 12-14 minutes, or until the middle springs back when you touch it, or a cake tester comes out clean.

To Assemble - Place a piece of jelly, a slice of seasonal fruit and a piece of cake per guest on a plate.

Tanuki:
Matsu's Old Fashioned

I typically ask Rowland, our insanely knowledgeable and talented bar manager, to make this with rum for me, because I much prefer rum to any liquor, but the staple whisky is perfect with it. A perfect study of quality ingredients, from the beverage perspective.

1/3oz Okinawan brown sugar syrup
2oz Mars Iwai blue label whiskey

Orange peels expressed on the entire inside and outside of the glass, twisted and garnished with pick

Master Recipes:

Krill Caramel

1tin Krill
50g Hon mirin
50g Usukuchi Shoyu
55g Sake
500g Okinawa Sugar
500g Mushroom Dashi
Mizunara and Salt TT

In a pan roast off krill and deglaze with sake, soy, and mirin. Add Okinawa sugar and mushroom dashi and reduce until desired thickness. Season with mizunara and salt.

Okinawan Brown Sugar Syrup

500g Okinawan Sugar
285g Water
1g Anise
2g Hojicha
1ea Kinome

Melt the Okinawan sugar in water with the anise. Once melted, steep in the hojicha and kinome for 1 hour. Strain.

Roast Chicken Dashi

5 yellow onions, charred
1c garlic cloves, whole
3 bunches green onions, bottoms only
1 Tbsp chili flake
20lb chicken bones, heavily roasted
4 sheets rishi kombu
3 bunches verbena
½ qt cilantro stems

4 sprigs kinome (optional)

Roast the chicken bones until deeply browned. Meanwhile, char the halved yellow onions on the grill. Once bones are roasted, combine with ingredients EXCEPT for kombu and herbs in stock pot, scraping the sheet trays with mirin to remove any cooked on bits and fill with water. Bring to a boil then reduce reduce heat to light simmer, just barely bubbling. Cook for minimum 4 hours, or overnight. Remove from heat and steep in herbs and kombu for 1 hour. Strain through chinois and reserve for later use.

Kinpira

3/4c dashi
2 Tbsp sake
1 Tbsp okinawan brown sugar
1 Tbsp mirin
1 1/2 Tbsp Usukuchi Shoyu

Slowly simmer until syrup, remove vegetable, slightly cool until thick, then glaze vegetable.

William Eick

1989 - Born

2006 - Began cooking career

2015 - First Executive Chef Position

2017 - Best Chef San Diego, Trillist Magazine

2018 - Best New Restaurant, 608 - Ranch and Coast Magazine

2018 - Best Farm to Table, 608 - Ranch and Coast Magazine

2021 - Opens Matsu

Matsu

2022 - Best New Restaurant - San Diego Magazine

2022 - Best Japanese Restaurant - San Diego Magazine

2023 - Best Japanese Restaurant - San Diego Magazine

2024 - Best Japanese Restaurant, Runner Up - San Diego Magazine

2025 - Essential 38 Restaurants - San Diego Eater

Our Suppliers

The Japanese Pantry
Japanese sugars, shoyu, vinegars, shio koji, sesame oil and seeds

Specialty Produce
Produce, AP flour, eggs

Ocean Fresh Seafood
Japanese fish, prawns, hon mirin

Asia International
Wagyu, whole duck

US Foods
Frying oil, paper goods

Joe Daly
Local rock fish

Concha Seafoods
Local rock fish, local tilefish

Tommy Gomes, Tunaville
Local fish

Prager Bros Bakery
Pastry flour for tempura

The Ecology Center
Produce

The Plot
Herbs

Nick Sakagami, Umitron
Japanese fish

MATSU

San Diego Terroir meets Japanese Cuisine

Published By: Self
Photography: Dee Sandoval
Written by: William Eick

Special Thanks: Keith Lord, Davin Waite, Michael Gardiner, Kevin Smith